Hello, Family Members,

Learning to read is one of the most important accomplishments of early childhood. **Hello Reader!** books are designed to help children become skilled readers who like to read. Beginning readers learn to read by remembering frequently used words like "the," "is," and "and"; by using phonics skills to decode new words; and by interpreting picture and text clues. These books provide both the stories children enjoy and the structure they need to read fluently and independently. Here are suggestions for helping your child *before*, *during*, and *after* reading:

Before

- Look at the cover and pictures and have your child predict what the story is about.
- Read the story to your child.
- Encourage your child to chime in with familiar words and phrases.
- Echo read with your child by reading a line first and having your child read it after you do.

During

- Have your child think about a word he or she does not recognize right away. Provide hints such as "Let's see if we know the sounds" and "Have we read other words like this one?"
- Encourage your child to use phonics skills to sound out new words.
- Provide the word for your child when more assistance is needed so that he or she does not struggle and the experience of reading with you is a positive one.
- Encourage your child to have fun by reading with a lot of expression . . . like an actor!

After

- Have your child keep lists of interesting and favorite words.
- Encourage your child to read the books over and over again. Have him or her read to brothers, sisters, grandparents, and even teddy bears. Repeated readings develop confidence in young readers.
- Talk about the stories. Ask and answer questions. Share ideas about the funniest and most interesting characters and events in the stories.

I do hope that you and your child enjoy this book.

> —Francie Alexander
> Reading Specialist,
> Scholastic's Learning Ventures

W9-CEE-019

To our first friends—the wolves.
—F.M.

To my wife, Tricia, and the rest of my
family: Thank you for enduring my
nonsense while I worked on this book.
—R.C.

ISBN: 0-439-08751-1

Text copyright © 2000 by Faith McNulty.
Illustrations copyright © 2000 by Richard Courtney.
All rights reserved. Published by Scholastic Inc.
SCHOLASTIC, HELLO READER, CARTWHEEL BOOKS and associated logos
are trademarks and/or registered trademarks of Scholastic Inc.

Library of Congress Cataloging-in-Publication Data

McNulty, Faith.
    The wolves ate my homework / by Faith McNulty; illustrated by Richard Courtney.
    p. cm. — (Hello reader! Level 4)
    "Cartwheel books."
    Summary: A boy learns about wolves when he accompanies his brother to a wildlife park to shoot a film about these ancestors of the pet dogs of today.
    ISBN 0-439-08751-1 (pbk.)
    1. Wolves Juvenile fiction. [1. Wolves Fiction] I. Courtney, Richard, 1955- 'ill. II. Title
III. Series: Hello reader! science Level 4.
    PZ10.3.M215Re 2000
    [E]—dc21   99-41359
                                                                            ⊦ CIP

12 11 10 9 8 7 6 5 4 3 2 1   00 01 02 03 04
                        Printed in the U.S.A.
                        First printing, February 2000

The Wolves Ate My Homework

by Faith McNulty

Illustrated by Richard Courtney

Hello Reader! Level 4

Cartwheel
·B·O·O·K·S· ®

SCHOLASTIC INC.

New York   Toronto   London   Auckland   Sydney
Mexico City   New Delhi   Hong Kong

My brother, Ben, loves wolves.
He says wolves are one of the most peaceable
animals in the world and one of the smartest.

Ben makes wildlife films.
Last summer he had a chance to work with
a pack of wolves at a wildlife park.
He asked me to be his helper.

I was thrilled, but my mother had doubts. "Is it really safe?" she asked. "I've always thought of wolves as dangerous. Don't they attack people?"

"No," Ben said. "Wild wolves are scared of people and run away if they see someone."

"Are these wolves tame?" my mother wanted to know.

"Not exactly," Ben said. "They aren't pets, but they are used to having people around. They were born in captivity at the park." Mom still worried.

"Do you go right into their cage?" she asked.

"I go near them, but there is no cage," Ben told her. "They live in a huge yard—a couple of acres—with a fence all around. They won't hurt you as long as you don't bother them."

Mom turned to me.

"What about school?" she asked.

"I'll only miss one day," I said, "and I'll take my homework with me."

Mom agreed to let me go, but made me promise to get all my homework done.

I promised.

Later that day Ben and I went for a walk
with my dog, Sasha.
She is beautiful — with soft fur and pointed
ears that wigwag, telling me how she feels.

"If you understand wolves," Ben said, "it is
easier to understand why dogs do the things
they do."
He explained that dogs are descended from
wolves that were adopted by humans,
perhaps as long ago as a thousand years.

"I can imagine a hunter killing a mother wolf,"
Ben said, "and bringing the puppies home.
Wolf puppies are easily tamed. Probably the
children played with them, and they became
family pets."

Ben told me that, of all wild animals, wolves
are best suited to live with humans.
Wolves and people have a lot in common.
Both are predators.
Wolves hunt to survive.
So did our early ancestors.
Like us, wolves hunt in a group or pack
and share what they kill.
The most important likeness between us
is the way wolves live in families, always close
and ready to care for each other.

This instinct for cooperation made tame wolves
useful to people in hunting, and guarding
their homes.
Eventually, tame wolves became a normal part
of life in many parts of the world.

After hundreds of years, these wolves became
very different from their ancestors.
People called them dogs.
"Most dogs don't look like wolves anymore,"
Ben said, "but there is still a lot of wolf
inside them."

Ben pointed out the wolf-like things about
Sasha.

First of all, the way she loves me.

She always wants to be with me: to walk with
me, ride in the car, lie at my feet, and sleep in
my bed.

Sasha's love for me, Ben said, comes from the
way wolves live together and depend on
each other.

A wolf alone is miserable.

A pack of wolves is led by the strongest male and his mate.

Their puppies stay with them even after they are grown.

Most of the wolves in a pack are related to each other.

A wolf pack is held together by strong feelings of loyalty.

Wolves mate for life.

If one of a pair is trapped, its mate will stay by its side.

If a wolf becomes too old or sick to hunt, the others bring it food.

When a wolf dies, the pack shows its sadness by howling.

Puppies are the pride and joy of the whole pack,
but wolves avoid having too many.
The leader and his mate have only one litter
a year.
The other wolves do not mate, but share in
raising the leader's puppies.

When the puppies are old enough to eat meat,
the others bring it to them.
Wolves carry meat by swallowing a piece whole
and bringing it up in the den.
This sounds disgusting, but the meat comes out
fresh and clean.
The puppies say thanks with squeals and lots
of kisses.

That evening, Ben showed us films to
illustrate how "human" wolves can be.
Like the father of a family, the top wolf is
respected by all the others.
Each wolf in a pack also has its place; there is
seldom any need to fight.
An argument about rank can be settled with
"body language."

A hard stare from a high-ranking wolf means
"Don't do that."
The other wolf will apologize by bowing
its head and looking away.
When two wolves argue, the higher-ranking
wolf holds its tail high.
If the other agrees to take second place, it
crouches with its tail low.
It may lick the other's mouth and even roll over
on its back.

There were once wolves almost everywhere in the world.
Today, after centuries of killing, very few remain.

Wolves were safe in America until the first white settlers came.
The Native Americans had no sheep or cows and lived peacefully with wolves.

But the newcomers brought all sorts of domestic animals that wolves found easy prey.
To protect their flocks, the settlers killed as many wolves as possible.
In most areas, the killing went on until there were none left to kill.

Today, wild wolves still survive only in the
northern wilderness.

Wolves in the United States are protected by law,
except in the state of Alaska, where they are still
being hunted and killed.

What has changed recently is that now many
people believe wolves have a place in nature
and do their best to protect them from hunters.

With Mom's permission, Ben and I started off
early the next day.

I kissed Sasha good-bye and told her I was
going to visit her ancestors.

It was a long drive and I managed to get my
homework done in the car.

At the wildlife park, we parked outside the
wolf yard.
It was a large area with grass and trees.
I looked through a chain-link fence and saw
my first wolf.
It looked like a big, gray dog curled up asleep.

As we came near, the wolf jumped to its feet.
It stared at us, ears pricked.

"That's Chief," Ben said. "He's the top dog—
the leader."
Chief was big.
He had long, slender legs and a long, bushy tail.
His gray eyes watched us with a proud stare
that made me feel his wildness.
Now the other wolves, resting here and there,
got up and gathered close to Chief.

Ben went to the fence and put his hand
against the wire.
The big wolf sniffed it.
I put out my hand and he sniffed mine, too.

Another wolf came near.
"That's Princess, his mate," Ben said.
"They have puppies in the den."
He pointed to a pile of boulders that made
a cave.
Ben opened the gate and slipped inside.
I picked up his camera bags and my bookbag
and followed.

As we walked toward the den, Chief and
Princess followed at our heels.
The others kept their distance.

Ben picked a spot to set up his camera.
"Don't go too near the den," he warned.
"They might not like it."

While Ben fussed with a camera, I sat on the
ground watching the wolves.
There were a dozen of them in the pack.
No two were exactly alike.
Their colors varied from black to
tawny yellow.

After a few minutes, the wolves lost interest
in us and wandered away.
Two of them began to play.
They wrestled the way dogs do, pawing each
other and pretending to bite.
It was fun to watch.
Playing a game of chase, they ran like the wind
and made quick, graceful turns.
Their long, bushy tails seemed to float
behind them.

Ben recognized these two as young wolves,

a brother and sister named Peter and Wendy.

Peter was almost black.

Wendy was a soft gray.

Ben began filming them.

He had several cameras.

As one ran out of film, he picked up another.

My job was to keep them all loaded.

Soon Princess went into the den, and we heard
squeals of delight from inside.
Ben said it must be suppertime for the puppies.
He aimed his camera at the entrance.

A moment later, Princess came out with three
puppies toddling after her.
They were round and fuzzy — as cute as only
puppies can be.
Their mother lay down on the grass, and they
swarmed over her, licking her face and
nuzzling for milk.

Peter and Wendy were interested in the scene
and came near, as though they wanted to play
with the puppies.
A stare and a soft growl from Princess
stopped them.

Then Peter and Wendy turned their attention
to me, circling around me as I sat on the grass.
They seemed to want to come closer, but didn't
quite dare.
Peter bowed in front of me.
With his mouth half open, he made a "play face,"
inviting me to join him in a game.

I was shaking my head to say *No, I'm busy,*
when something hit me in the back.

It was Wendy, snatching my cap off my head
as she ran by.

With her prize in her mouth, she ran circles
around me.

Her laughing eyes seemed to dare me to chase
her and take it away.

I leaped to my feet.
Without thinking, I yelled, "Drop that!"
as I would have at Sasha.
Of course, Wendy paid no attention.

Now Peter joined in and snatched the cap
from Wendy.
I watched helplessly as they tore it in two.
Peter got the biggest piece.
He tossed it a few times and then lay down
to chew it.

"Say good-bye to your hat!" Ben said.
He was grinning as he filmed the mischievous
pair. "Sorry, I forgot to tell you that these guys
love to steal stuff. The first time I met them
they ate my best gloves."

Then something worse happened.

I had left my bookbag on the ground.
Wendy spotted it, darted in, and grabbed it.

The sight of her dragging it away was more
than I could stand.
Without stopping to think, I ran after her
and dived for the bag.
I got a grip on it, but Wendy didn't let go.
We were in a tug of war.

I was so excited that I hardly heard Ben yelling
at me.
He was still taking pictures and at the same time
yelling, "Let go! Let go! Let her have it!"
I was too mad to be afraid. I kept hanging on.

Now Peter joined Wendy and the bag was
yanked out of my hands.
I saw it come apart.
The wolves were very excited, their eyes shining
with fun.
Papers began to fly.
A notebook was torn to shreds.

I must have been in a frenzy to do what I did next.

I grabbed one of the wolves by the tail.

It was Peter.

I tried to pull him off the bag.

He turned and snarled.

His eyes had a greenish shine, his hair was standing up, and his teeth bared.

Scared at last, I let go, but in the same second I was knocked down by a blow from another direction.

Flat on my back on the ground, I looked up
into the pale eyes of a huge, dark wolf.
It was Chief, standing over me, his open jaws
just a few inches from my face.
Peter was right beside him.

I remember seeing gleaming-white teeth, and
hearing deep, rumbling growls.
I heard Ben's voice saying, "Stay still!
Don't move!"

Rigid with fear, I closed my eyes and felt the
big wolf sniffing my face.
His cold, wet nose nuzzled my neck, poked
my ear, ruffled my hair.
My heart almost stopped.

When I opened my eyes, he was still standing
over me, staring down, as though trying to
decide whether to eat me in one bite or two.
I heard Ben's calm voice saying, "Take it easy.
It's okay. He's not mad. He won't hurt you
as long as you stay still."

Seconds ticked by.

Suddenly, the big wolf lost interest in me and walked away, leaving me on the ground.

I began to get up, but Peter moved in to sniff me and I lay still while his nose poked me here and there.

At last he moved off and I scrambled to my feet.

Ben was beside me, asking anxiously if
I was okay.
I said I was, and was surprised at how my
voice trembled.
I realized I was trembling all over.

Gripping my arm, Ben scolded me.
"What were you thinking?" he said.
"I thought you had more sense than to pull
a wolf by the tail. Even a dog will bite you
if you do a dumb thing like that."

I guess that's when I began to cry.
Ben stopped scolding.
He patted my back and rubbed my hair,
trying to make me feel better.

"I don't blame you for being scared," he said.
"It must have been an awful feeling looking into
the jaws of a wolf. You were lucky. He was just
restoring order. He's the boss here, and wolves
don't like fighting in the family."

I nodded and wiped my eyes.

Looking around, I saw that Peter and Wendy were lying down nearby.

Peter was chewing the bookbag as though it were a bone.

Wendy had a mangled notebook between her paws.

Beside her was a pile of paper shredded to confetti.

"My homework!" I wailed, looking at the wreckage. "I wanted to save my homework! What can I tell my teacher?"

"Never mind the homework," Ben said
soothingly. "We'll fix it somehow."
He began to laugh. "Tell your teacher that the
wolves ate it! I'll bet that's one excuse she's
never heard."
"She'll never believe me," I said.
"Show her the pieces," Ben advised.

Together, we picked up the scraps of paper and
stuffed them into a plastic bag.
The wolves ignored us as we packed up
our gear and left.

I was nervous going into class the next day.
My story sounded weird and hard to believe,
until I showed the class the chewed-up remains.
Then everyone laughed and wanted me to
tell more.

Mrs. Maccarone, our teacher, was forgiving.
She said I could replace the lost work with a
story about my visit to the wolves.

Here it is.
Believe it or not, I got an A.